WHO'S TIFFANY

A Trans-Child's Coming-Out Novella

EAST OAKLAND TIMES

THE CALIFORNIA DREAM

Foreward

Tiffany Rhiaunda Tooks is a post-operation (post-op) transgender woman of color living at Central California Women's Facility (CCWF) in Chowchilla, California. Ms. Tooks biography *Who's Tiffany? A Trans-Child's Coming-Out Novella* depicts in sketch the heartbreak and self-discovery integral to Tiffany's self-acceptance as a transgender female. *Who's Tiffany?* implicitly affirms transgender integrity through a narration of Tiffany's search for identity in a time and place hostile to transgender actualization and self-expression, working-class black American neighborhoods of Los Angeles during the late 1960s through the early 1980s.

While *Who's Tiffany?* is staggering with regard to the personal conflicts communicated, the end message endorses the character autonomy gained through courageous self-acceptance. A related and integral lesson of the novella is that hatred towards others, namely transgender persons, is not a defensible means to "normalize" the hated. Inflicting pain upon persons uniquely stitched with "uncommon" or "different" characteristics is neither productive nor beneficial; rather, intolerance of character and individuality is illustrative of disdain for the breadth and depth of human personality. On God's earth, humanity has come in a brilliant and daring diversity of forms and imprints. Tolerance is the teaching that we judge for ourselves and allow others to find themselves.

The momentum of modern-day California affirms the moral call to tolerate diversity in peoples, persons, and pursuits. Such a reality can only advance if citizens of every persuasion give ground to others. There cannot be a disagreement and dislike free social solution. However, on the foundation of perfect laws can human interactions create a tolerant social order. Choices on ways of being and value belong to the individual, similar to manner of worship. In this way can the mortal yet ever renewing human race find group purpose via individual destinies. Beneath the broad tolerance of personal freedom under law, contemporaries view the many and varying lights that composite the community firmament and draw toward one or another twinkling star.

The right to choose one's way of being is a privilege of maturity and self-responsibility; to be left alone is a right of liberty. By left alone, it is specifically meant "safe." Safety is security in person and property. No citizen can be denied this civic protection, nor must citizens seek much more, for seeking more unevenly distributes and offsets the general harmony founded in the equality of rights before the law. Even so, transgender people have historically possessed a distinct charism that has drawn unwanted aggression. To inculcate acceptance of transgender persons is proper for the general public's cognizance of citizen protections, the right to safety and security. Advocating for the transgender individual's right to move freely in the world without threats of violence is an advocation for all people of every distinct group of persons to exist in collective harmony.

Transgender identity freed from the closet increases in richness the character of human life. Humanity is blessed by persons who augment the tension on each of us to find ourselves and, for some, to accept others. The transgender individual testifies to the great good of being authentic to who one is and the mission for us each to discover that individual. Such a world is a viable ideal that requires a legal emphasis on all people's right to safety and a community will to unite as champions of shared freedom.

A future vision of tolerance in California: common decency becomes the norm; a valued and cherished social order sprouts roots bringing forth the blessings of culture; public and private behavior find their proper place; the obscene, the violent, and the corrupt retreat to the shadows; people go about their lives, living in their truth.

Tio MacDonald
Berkeley, CA
July 2020

PREFACE

When we live our lives based on the expectations of others, we are not living for ourselves. Not living our own lives brings about confusion, depression and the deprivation of our identities, individuality, and self-worth. To live for yourself is to become the authentic you that you are and to be the best you that you are. Being yourself and truly living your life will bring happiness, even if others disagree with the choices you have made on how you live your life. If living your life as you chose brings you loss from those who may disagree, just know that there is always much to gain in the wings waiting to greet you. Your strength is yourself! Just reach for it inside of you and extract it any time you feel you are about to give up or when you grow weak. Most importantly, never deny yourself the most important truth that we are entitled to - the right to be ourselves without apology.

Remember that your life is just that, it is yours and it is the only one that you get, so live it to the fullest.

My name is Tiffany and I am a transgender woman. My story is as unique as I am. I revealed myself, my true identity, when I was very young and it was not an easy thing to do. After going through years of struggle, years of confusion, doubt, pain, and despair, the type that no child should ever have to go through, I came to embrace just who I am. This is my story.

STRONG SOUTHERN ARMS

I WAS RAISED BY DIFFERENT FAMILY MEMBERS AT different times and stages of my childhood. My first memories are of being with my Aunt Maddie, who was my father's sister. She was a strong, confident, God-fearing, southern woman. She brought me to California in October of 1966. At that time, I was only six months old. She gave me undying love and care.

I never knew her as my aunt, but as my mother, being that she was the first person I recognized as a parental figure. She was very protective of me and never allowed anyone to scold or spank me no matter what it was that I had done. Whenever someone tried, she would raise up her imposing frame and, in a tone that could put fear into the devil, speak the words that always made me feel safe, "Don't you touch my baby!"

Then, like any large animal in the wild, she would shield me with her body, letting all know that they had to come through her to get to me.

I never felt, at any time, while living with her, that I was not the star in her eyes that dazzled her to delight. I was her great joy and the grand prize she always proclaimed. I love her so much for the love she gave me without ceasing, every single day of my life that she had me in her protective care.

I always felt free living with Aunt Maddie and her home was always warm and comforting. I recall an early memory of my life when I was around five years old. I was outside playing with a friend of mine who lived across the street. Like all kids at that age, we were innocent in our intentions and just having fun. My friend was a little girl of the same age as I was, and the two of us playing together never once seemed wrong or odd. In my mind, being with my friend and acting like her was as "normal" as normal could be.

My Aunt Maddie also had my teenage cousin James Henry living with us. Now James was a young jock. He was always quick to flex his "alpha male" persona at me, especially on those occasions when he felt as if I were invading his personal space. He also did this whenever he became agitated about something he disliked me doing. Even so, my Aunt Maddie was always only a dash away to defend me against his temper.

Well, on this particular day, James came home agitated about something, saw me playing, and ordered me to get up and go into the house. "What's wrong with you? You're out here playing with girls like some damn sissy! I'm gonna teach you how to be a tough boy. You ain't no girl!" He shouted and shoved me through the front door and into the living room.

I instantly bolted into an all-out run towards my Aunt Maddie, who was in the kitchen cooking dinner. James was right on my heels, determined to snatch me up before I reached the safety of her arms. Just over my shoulder I could hear him yelling at me, "You little punk!" I let out an ear-piercing scream as I felt him closing the distance between us. Mentally I asked myself what it was that I had done to him to cause him to hate me so much.

My Aunt Maddie turned around just as I reached her. "What is going on? Why are y'all running through my house yelling like you're not raised to have good sense?" She looked at both of us, seeking an answer. All the while, she instinctively shielded me from his reach.

James looked at me with a scowl on his face and then at Aunt Maddie. His anger was evident. Only God knows what he would have done to me if not for Aunt Maddie saving me. "He's out there playing with a girl like he's a girl too! So, I made him come in and he ran like a little punk."

In a flash, Aunt Maddie rose up over James and as serious as I had ever seen her be, said in a firm and terrifying tone, "He's a child, James! My child! And, if he wants to play with the girls, let him be! Do you hear me?" She stared down at James as if daring him to defy her words.

James cowered while he also tried to make the point that by babying me, Aunt Maddie was making me soft. He said that he could toughen me up. He kept going on and on about how she was enabling my behavior until Aunt Maddie grew tired of hearing him.

"You will not put a single finger on my baby. Do you hear me, boy? Or, I will hurt you, James. That is my baby, my child, and I say he can play with whoever he is happy to play with. So leave him the heck alone and let him be!" She yelled her point at him. James knew that her word was law.

BIG GIRLS DON'T CRY

THAT IS A TIME IN MY LIFE I OFTEN REVISIT WHEN thinking about if my family was aware of my differences in how I felt. Did they know or understand that I was a girl who did not recognize that she was born a boy? Did my wonderful, beautiful, loving, and protective Aunt Maddie know that my feminine behavior was more than me going through a childhood stage?

I know that this was the exact period in my childhood when I came to know that I did not identify with being the boy that my family members knew or saw me as. This was a time that I wanted to present the image of myself that I was deeply convinced, and without a doubt knew, that I indeed was a girl.

At the age of six, I moved to my mother and her husband's home. A deep urge and yearning rooted inside of me to express the girl who I should have been born at birth. The internal demand to express myself fed on my spirit like a pride of lions feeds upon a freshly killed carcass - tearing to shreds a vibrant life that once existed and roamed freely.

I refer to this period of my life, sadly, as being the worst I have had to experience. This was a time that I would not live over again. It was awful and painful in ways that are too hard to describe. It was so severe. I went through stages of depression. I started to show irrational behaviors that led to violent outbursts and the start of criminal behavior. I lived through an emotional tumult caused by having to hide my true self from my family, who were trying hard as they could to figure out what in the world was wrong with me. It took a sorrowful toll on my spirit. I could not explain things to them because I only knew it to be what it was: in my mind I was a girl and my body was not showing it. I believed that they would not understand and that they'd punish me and probably would not want me anymore.

This led me deeper into the pits of personal sadness. I had no one to save me. I felt as if no one cared about me and that they all thought that I was psychotic and in need of both therapy and medication to calm my behavior. It was like they were trying to bring me back down to their idea of normality so that I could be their 'good little boy' that they all wanted me to be.

Little did they know that that was the cause for all of my issues. I wanted to scream, "I'm not a boy! I don't want to be a boy, so stop forcing it upon me and just let me be the girl that I am. This is causing me to suffer a terrible existence, so much so that I feel like I want to die." Yet as I said, I did not mention any of these things. Instead, I kept myself, my true self, wrapped up tightly and protected within.

I endured this period of tormented hell from 1972-1978. It was six years of a time that I still, to this day, have trouble sharing without being crippled by the pain that I, as a child, endured. That pain for me was greater than receiving the life sentence in prison that I am currently serving.

Leaving my Aunt Maddie's care to go back and live with my biological mother was a difficult adjustment for me to process and accept. My mother's name is Ruby Nell Jenkins. She was beautiful in a more youthful and modern sort of way than my Aunt Maddie. My mother was short. She was only five-feet five-inches tall.

She had the most beautiful smile that I ever saw. She held a confidence and was very sure of herself, owning everything about herself with pride. I came to love and admire her. Yet, for all of that which she was, there was a nightmare who accompanied her. That nightmare was named George Johnson.

George was a sharply dressed man who was very difficult to read. One could not predict what attitude he would spring upon you at any given moment. Now, I will give him credit as a man for being a dependable provider for the needs of his family. Further, while I was not his biological child, as were my siblings, he did not treat me any differently. But, I can't have much more praise for a man who was abusive to my mother. I was mentally traumatized by all of the violence he unleashed upon her in front of me. Not only did he not care about the abuse he was putting my mom through, he never gave a thought to how witnessing his violence was affecting me at such a young age. My developing mind was trying hard to process and make sense of the horrors I would witness. His actions were nothing like my Aunt Maddie's.

My mother always loved watching me dance and would often put on one of her vinyl records and have me dance and entertain her. I rejoiced in it. It was during those times that I always felt the closest to her. I danced with sheer delight and she would often join in with me. George did not equally rejoice with how my mother bonded with me and, like most of the men I have encountered, spoke many belittling things about me. My feelings would instantly collapse the moment George set foot in the room. He always had a stupid or shameful comment about me dancing. "Why is that boy shaking like some damn girl?" Or, he would say to me, "Go sit your little sissy ass down somewhere." Defeated in my spirit, I often wished for a rock to crawl behind and hide there forever. He effectively destroyed my soul with each syllable of his cruel, targeted words.

Another thing that George hated about me was my hair. He always made that known without giving care as to how his words made me feel. "That boy don't need to have all that damn hair on his head. He's too old for all that girly ass hair. You ought to let me get him a haircut." My mother, bless her heart, in her attempts to protect me, even though she couldn't protect herself from this aggressive man she loved, would defend me. She regularly stopped him from trying to cut my long locks and force me to have what he called 'man's hair,' which was a short haircut. Still, try as she might, George already had his mind made up. He was going to cut my hair no matter what my mother thought or how she felt. Besides, no woman in George's world challenged his words, or they were subject to be beaten for displaying defiance, something he detested.

I was awakened one Saturday morning along with my stepbrother Prince, who was George's son from another woman named Virginia. George, in a hushed tone, instructed us to get washed up and dressed; then he quietly took us out of the house as my mother slept in her room. She worked all week at a nursing home for the elderly and slept in late on Saturdays if she didn't have any errands to run.

We went down to the car and George drove off to a barber's college in the downtown area of Long Beach. I didn't protest even though I had an idea of what was about to happen. Nor did I cry when I was told to get into the barber's chair. George stood behind me, instructing the barber to cut my hair into a buzz cut style. I recall how he seemed to get a thrill as he watched the clumps of hair fall off my head and onto the floor. After it was all over, and once Prince had his hair cut as well, we left.

George treated us both to an ice cream cone and, as proud as he could be, said to me, "Now that is how a boy is supposed to look." I didn't express any feelings as we headed back home.

Now we knew not to bother my mother as she slept, but as we entered the house, I ran straight to her room, yelling out in an ear-piercing pitch that only a child in distress could make, "Ruby! Ruby! Ruby! Look at me. Look at my new haircut." She was lying on her side, facing away from me. In an irritated voice, she finally spoke. "What is wrong with you coming in her making all that damn noise waking me up, boy?"

I stood there, waiting for her to see me. "Look! I got a haircut," I said. She finally started focusing on my words and sat up to get a real good look at me. A frown crossed her face.

"What have you done to your hair?" She asked.

My response was, "George." She jumped from her bed and threw on her robe in a single motion. My mother strode past me and entered the living room where George sat with Prince watching television.

"What have you done to my baby's hair George?" She snapped at him in anger. "I cut that damn boy's hair. He don't need to be having all that damn hair on his head. He's a boy and you need to stop treating him like he is a damn girl and babying his ass anyway. That's why he acts like he do now."

My mother's reaction was one that was filled with rage. She spat her words at him. "That's my child! You had no right to cut off his hair!"

George replied obstinately, "Well, I did it!"

I can still feel the depths of all his words as they dug into the chambers of my heart and mind. They anchored themselves there and became a painful and blistering memory.

All I recall from there was a blur of movement. George beat my mother so that she ended up both bloody and swollen as if she had survived a car accident. This was his chilling and dangerous reminder that he brokered no defiance.

He stood over my mother's broken frame as she tried to shield herself from additional punches and kicks. "Don't you ever in your life tell me what I don't have the right to do! Do you understand me?"

"Yes, George."

He stepped around my mother, grabbed his hat and coat and left the house with an angry slam of the door. I became accustomed to hearing them arguing and fighting throughout the years of living under George's roof.

———————

THERE WAS a time that I refer to as the second happiest of my childhood. This is when I found myself living in the same household as my sister Tracy Johnson. We lived in the home of a woman named Flora Mae Johnson, who we affectionately called "Granny." It was the second happiest because living with Aunt Maddie remained the first. By this time, Aunt Maddie had married and moved to Michigan.

Living with Granny was a beautiful blend of love and peace. It was harmony. She loved me and always made me feel special. She was one of my greatest teachers in life. She taught me things that later on would prepare me to live on my own and not depend on anyone else for survival. She taught Tracy and me how to cook from scratch. We had a garden in the backyard that we worked in to bring us delicious fresh vegetables.

Further, never once did Granny scold me or cause me to feel as if I were wrong for playing with girls or their toys. George never tolerated such behavior and probably would have tried to kill me if he ever witnessed me playing with the toys of any girl.

Living with my sister Tracy, who was a year younger than me, was too perfect. I love her like the air I need to breathe. Yes, she is my sister, but we quickly became best friends as well. We did everything together and I never once was made to feel as if I were different. Although I was always introduced to people as her brother, I comfortably felt like we were sisters. When we played together and imitated women at church that we admired, I felt accepted. We never copied the men.

I was allowed to be me, the true me that I am on the inside, without any judgment or pressure. And, without the negativity of "not acting like a boy." I was free to live as a kid and be happy. Granny always encouraged me to be "true to self."

One day Granny received a phone call that informed her that Aunt Maddie had passed away in her sleep. I was both devastated and confused. It was hard for me to process that this loving and caring woman, one who had basically been my mother, was now gone forever. Granny took her time and explained it all to me in a way that I could process. I cried and felt like I wanted to die too so that I could go and be with Aunt Maddie forever. To this day, I still miss her and the love and care she gave to me.

Not too long after that, the day came when life as I knew it unraveled around me and set my feet on a path of destruction that would have me experience the loss of everything. Tracy and I were playing in the front yard when a car pulled up and parked. I saw a tall black woman approach the house. She was dressed nicely. She smiled in acknowledgment of us as she briskly strode past us and went to the front door.

She knocked and after a few moments was greeted by Granny who allowed her inside. Some time passed as Tracy and I played until Granny called for Tracy to come inside. I, of course, followed her in. The woman was sitting across from Granny with papers in her hand that she had pulled from a folder.

Granny was giving answers to the woman's questions. I sat quietly wondering who she was and why she was asking so many questions. Why did she want to know about Tracy's care? I didn't understand how anyone could question Granny at all about her love and care for my sister, whom she had raised from birth. Granny's home was filled with love and happiness, not chaos and violence. Being with her was like being in heaven.

There were no worries or problems that Granny could not fix and make right.

The woman made me feel very uncomfortable and I decided that I did not like her. I was getting a lot of negative vibes from her, and she made me feel nervous. She kept flipping through the papers in her hand then turned her attention to me. She asked Granny who I was and Granny told her that Tracy and I were sister and brother.

The lady sat there for a moment and everything was completely silent. My bad vibes towards her grew stronger as the silence grew heavier and thicker. She looked up and told Granny that she had to place me back with my mom. Even though Granny told her that living with my mom was not a good option for me, the lady said that I could not stay there without the proper legal authority. She went on to say that she was going to report my presence in the house to her agency.

As she stood up, she gave me a dry look and an even drier apology. "Sorry," she said. Once she left, we sat together in more silence. The kind of silence that felt as if you were suffocating in it. It soon became nearly unbearable and I asked Granny what did the woman mean? Granny, in her ever-loving way, explained that I had to go back to my mom and George.

I sat in total shock, reviving mental remembrances of the horrors I had witnessed and experienced living there. I did not want to live through them again. I felt fear wrap itself around me in a tight grip. I was terrified of what George would do to me and I told Granny that I wanted to stay with her. As sweetly as she could, Granny, in trying to ease my displeasure, made it clear to me that the situation was out of her hands; if she were able to, she would keep me forever.

I burst into anger and defiance. I looked at both Granny and Tracy and declared that if they made me go back, they would never see me again. Tears of pain and anguish ran freely down my face. Sadly, those heated words spoken from the mouth of a confused child became a promise that I came to make good on.

BREAKING WINDOWS

I HAVE A SISTER NAMED SONYA AND A BROTHER NAMED Howard who are younger than I am. We call my brother Howard, Dion, because that is his middle name. My mother had four kids with me being the oldest, yet no longer being the only child, did not make things any easier for me. Now I love my mother and know that she gave the depths of herself to make me a happy child, but she could not save me from the traumatizing fear that of the man she chose to love. Even though it caused great suffering to her children, suffering that has had a long-lasting effect on all of our lives, she could not leave George.

Once again, I fell into a state of depression as my home life was filled with violence. My siblings were continually crying out of fear. I hated it. I was no longer a child because I had to quickly learn to be there for my brother and sister. I had to comfort them as I had once been comforted by both Aunt Maddie and Granny. I had to shield them the best I could from the wrath that rained down like a flood from that maniac George.

My grades dropped and I started to run away from home in the hope of never returning or never being found. I would wander around with no particular place to go until I got picked up by the police who were out looking for me. My once happy self was replaced with a person filled with bitterness, anger, frustration, confusion, and sadness. I became reclusive and quiet. I was frequently asked what was wrong with me, as opposed to what was wrong with the environment that I had to live in. I replied by saying, "Nothing."

The truth was, I was tired of trying to gain clarity and understand the home I was in. I was also struggling to understand the hidden feelings I was battling every day. I was a boy and I didn't feel right within myself about it. I knew that everyone around me was saying and teaching me to be a boy, but it just did not feel like I was that person. I was never that little boy that they all wanted.

It hurt because I could not even talk to my mother about what I was going through. I had no guidance. I didn't want to disappoint anyone and I tried to do everything that was expected of me, just to please them. The truth of the matter is, I felt so deeply inside that I was meant to be and was a girl that I began to harbor resentment towards everyone, including myself.

At the age of nine, I was overwhelmed by how I was feeling, so I started seeking ways to escape from the living environment I was in. I was trapped living the life of a lie, that I didn't even want to live anymore. I could not take any more of the negative comments that were being hurled at me. No one had a clue as to the toll it was taking on me. I wondered what was wrong with me and why the body I was in felt like it did not belong to me. I did not identify as being correct and had no idea what 'dysphoria' was or even meant. All I knew was pain and suffering.

Despite all this, there were happy times when I enjoyed the comfort of family, especially when we had "movie week" together. We would head downtown to the big theatre and enjoy the latest movie. It was during those times that we were treated to a moment of peace and the terrifying violence experienced at home was nowhere to be seen. We would also go out and eat dinner as a family.

As I have said before, George was a great provider for his family and he taught me practical life skills I used to survive. Both my George and my mother did their best to provide us all with a proper and decent life. It is just that I never truly felt safe because of the violence he unleashed at any moment.

Eventually, I started to come undone. My negative behavior increased and I began criminal-type activities. I was arrested by the Long Beach Police. It brought my mom great pain, disappointment, and embarrassment when she had to pick me up from the station. She couldn't believe that a nine-year-old child, let alone her child, could be so violent and bad.

I hated having to add to her already stressful life with my getting into trouble. It could be truthfully stated that I was out of control. There were more arrests made and she began to feel she did not have the answer as to what to do with or for me. I know that she often wondered what had happened to the good little kid that she knew that I could be. My heart will always bear the pain and scars of all the problems, stress, and worry that I caused her. But, I had always felt that she could never truly understand what was really wrong. No one could! And, because of this, my violent actions continued. Finally, my behavior couldn't be tolerated any longer, so I was placed in juvenile detention, where an entirely new world was opened up and introduced to me.

WILD CHILDS

JUVENILE DETENTION WAS A CONFINED PLACE WITH LONG hallways, big, empty rooms where you were locked in most of the time, and there were more loud-mouthed kids than I had ever seen in my life. This was a place that the police referred to as "The Big House." They were attempting to scare me like I was part of a scared straight program so that I would get my act together. But, little did they know, being in that place helped me find answers to the issues I had been struggling with for all the short years of my childhood. For the first time, I saw what appeared to me as young girls, but were actually kids that were born as boys. I instantly knew that they were just like me. They were boys who were meant to be girls. They seemed to be living as themselves without care about the opinions of anyone. They were free. They owned who they were. They were doing and being all that I wanted but was too afraid to do.

I admit that I secretly watched everything they did and I observed everything with a sense of awe and wonder. Whenever we had recreational time, I would make sure that I could watch. I had such envy inside of me, the kind like I had never felt before. I wanted to have that freedom for myself, but the fear of what my family would think if they knew my secret, caused me to suppress my feelings deeper into the chambers of my heart. As a result, I continued to suffer from my gender identity.

One day during our recreational gym period I was approached, for the first time ever, by one of the "girls," as I learned that they were called, named La' Tasha. I was 10 years old and this was my first up-close encounter with her. I was more than a little nervous, yet I was also excited. She was being very friendly and trying to engage me in a conversation, but I was being guarded. I had worn a mask over who I truly was for so long that it was not in any way easy to let the mask slip. And, as such, I wore a tough exterior. I made sure that I acted like a street kid. I acted like a little thug.

Now I had made a point of letting all the other boys around me know that I was no pushover, no punk, and definitely not a sissy. So, when La' Tasha came up to me and said hi, and all of the other guys started laughing, I quickly reacted.

"What the hell is so funny?" I snapped in a defensive tone that let them know that I didn't find anything at all funny. Now, I don't know exactly when "never showing weakness" became my greatest survival skill, but I brought it to the forefront immediately. It had brought me respect amongst gang members, thugs, and all the bullies that the kids deemed as dangerous and violent. At age ten, imagine that! I stood and challenged anyone, letting them know that I was going to fight. I had already fought my way to status and reputation as a tough kid. Some of the other kids were already looking up to me or for me to help them when they had issues with the other boys that they feared.

So, when the guys told me that they were laughing at me because La'Tasha had spoken to me, I knew that I could not show any signs or form of weakness. "Shut the hell up!" I demanded. They saw that I was getting angry and began to show me what I knew I would never show any of them, they showed me submissiveness. They showed me that they were afraid and weak.

And, like every time it was exposed to me, I exploited it to the fullest. I used it to boost my own status and to cover up my hidden secret.

They started letting me know that they were only joking and started asking me not to take the things they were saying seriously. They said words such as, "We were only joking cause that homosexual said that you were cute." I feigned my anger and let them all know not to play with me about her stepping to me. Secretly, deep down on the inside, I was thanking her for that day. However, my behavior towards her was anything but appreciative.

As the weeks went on, La' Tasha would say something to get my attention or be near me whenever our paths crossed. Eventually, I confronted her about messing with me. To my surprise, instead of backing down or showing fear like a lot of the other kids did, she was defiant and clearly not fearful of me. La'Tasha gave me a look as to say that she could not believe that I had the nerve to speak to her as I had done. She leaned her tall frame down to bring us face to face and to show her visible agitation and displeasure at my tough act. No matter what any of the other people thought, La'Tasha was not buying it. "So you think that you are tough and all that, huh? Well, you may have these boys fooled, but

I know who you are! You're just like me except you're hiding in your musty ass closet too scared to come out because you know that you are a coward. You want to come out and be as real as me. So, don't try me trade! Or, should I say Ms. Tooks?" She popped her fingers in a fashion that I had never seen before as if she were cracking a whip, then stepped off to wherever she was heading.

I stood there, dumbfounded. La' Tasha said that she knew my secret. But how? I had always made sure that I never exposed my inner self to anyone in any sort of way. Her words bugged the hell out of me. I began talking to her just to find out how she knew what my inner self was. She didn't seem to pose a threat and always seemed supportive to me and my secret. She told me that things would be alright and that I did not have to continue to be tortured by the secret that I had held in for so long. She assured me that I was not the only person in the world who was going through what I felt.

As such, I slowly began to open up to her more and more during our private conversations. It was during one of these talks that she showed me by her actions, that I could trust her wholeheartedly. La' Tasha was so helpful in so many ways with all of the knowledge and understanding she gave me. She helped me release so much of the built-up pressure inside of me. This, in turn, gave me peace in the fact of knowing that there was nothing wrong with me. And, for that, I am eternally grateful to her.

GOD GAVE ME A FRIEND

In 1978, I was placed in a group home in Compton, California. It was run by a woman known as Momma Tee. She was a very suspicious, judgmental, and stern woman who had a "take no shit from anyone" attitude. She read the rules of how she ran her house as if they were laws that Congress had enacted. She left no room for questioning who was the sole authority and who ran the house.

We never got along because, at that time in my life, I had a disregard for any form of authority or authoritative figure. It was a point where I thought that everyone was against me. Momma Tee was determined and adamant that she was going to be the one to break my spirit and have me fall in line. She was determined to bring me to total submission to her will, and I was just as adamant and determined not to succumb to what she wanted. I took her challenge as served. In my mind, it was definitely game on! The two of us clashed and butted heads at every single turn.

At the time when I first entered the home, she gave me the tour of the house and showed me to the room where I would be staying. I was to have a roommate named Mark. Mark was at school, so I spent a while checking out the room. In my assessment, I sensed a feminine quality and thought it odd for someone who was named Mark. He seemed to be much neater than most of the boys I knew. I had been told that he was twelve years old.

I noticed his record player and records and went to check them out. He had records by Donna Summers, Stacy Lattisaw, and Dianna Ross, amongst many others. I thought that it was a weird selection of music for a boy to be listening to. I was both curious and anxious to meet this person and I wondered if the two of us would be able to get along. I was not going to be pushed over by anyone just because I was now the new kid in the house. I understood that I was going to have to assert myself from the moment we met.

Later that afternoon, while watching T.V. in the living room with Momma Tee, Mark came home from school. Momma Tee introduced us to each other. Mark was short, light-skinned, and had the mannerisms of a girl. I tried studying him without being too obvious about what I was doing. Momma Tee made sure to explain to me that Mark was "different" and that she expected me to be respectful of him and to be nice to him. She didn't want me to be bullying or trying to take advantage of him in any kind of way.

Little did she or Mark know that secretly, I was happy that Mark was as he was, a girl in the shape of a boy. He was just like me. I asked myself the odds that I would get to be so close to someone who was every-thing that I could not openly be? It felt right to me. It was as if some higher power had heard my silent pleas that my soul had been crying out for as long as I could remember and gave me the answers that I needed in Mark.

The two of us quickly became friends and spent a lot of time talking and laughing together. We would some-times talk ourselves to sleep. In fact, we did that almost every night. I found myself so happy to have Mark as my new best friend. I remember one night we were lying in our separate beds and Mark was talking in such a caring way. He was letting me know that he had been in my shoes. He knew that the pair I had on did not fit my feet, just like the ones he had once worn did not fit his. He said that he had to go and get himself a new pair, ones that actually fit the feet of his life - a pair that was comfortable for him.

At first, I didn't understand what he was saying, but then it dawned on me that he was talking about our personalities. He was talking about being true to who you are. He suddenly asked me a question during our conversation. "Why are you so scared?" I didn't exactly know what he meant and I was not sure where the conversation was going. As far as I had shown him and everyone else, I was not afraid of anything for I had been vigilant to keep my persona up. I decided to answer, "Afraid of what?" Without any hesitation, he continued, "Of being who you really feel that you are. Wouldn't you feel better being free to be the girl that you are?" He paused, then pressed further without waiting for my answer. "Everybody knows my tea. I don't hide myself to or for anybody. My mother accepts me just as I am. You don't have to be afraid and be alone." I was stunned that we were actually talking about this. I had never spoken out loud to anyone about me and I didn't know what to say. Mark and I had spoken in the past as if we were speaking about someone else; never had we talked openly about me. I remember exactly how I felt when he said this. I didn't want to lie to my friend and I know that it was something that I really needed to stop holding in because I was feeling like a dam about to burst. I had only revealed my female truth to him with my actions and not my words. I knew that somehow by actually speaking the words out loud, I would give life to my inner self. Doing so would bring about an entirely new change.

To his credit, Mark made me feel relaxed and comfortable. It never occurred to me that the "female" who had been longing to come out of me would reveal herself by simply having the candid dialogue we were having. Knowing that I could not lie to Mark, I started doing some thing that I had never done in front of anyone, I started crying. Instead of making fun of me or laughing, Mark spoke: "Please don't cry," he whispered. "I know what it feels like being scared and hiding, but you don't have to anymore." He said in a soothing voice. I cried into my pillow, allowing my soul to be washed clean by my tears. The pillow soaked up those tears and muffled the sounds of anguish that poured out of me. I unleashed all of those painful and confusing years from the deepest part of my being. I told Mark that I didn't know what to do and why I couldn't tell my family. I told him that I feared being alone and unloved. I didn't want to be by myself, where no one wanted me.

In my opinion, Mark was wise far beyond his years and seemed like he knew all of what adults knew about life's issues. "Don't worry, my mother will love you just like she does me. You are my best friend. You are my sister. And I will tell my mother how much you need her. I promise you that I will. I just hate seeing you like this." Telling Mark my truth was big for me. I couldn't even tell La' Tasha all of my struggles with my gender when the two of us had all of our discussions. While talking with Mark, I learned new words to assign to all of the inner feelings. I also learned how to do research about what I was going through and what it was identified as.

———

WHEN I BEGAN MY INVESTIGATIONS, I was excited and interested, hoping that I could pinpoint with an accurate understanding of what and who I was and why I was like I was. All of the information that I never knew existed for my feelings was being revealed to me. It became clear that there were people all over the world, many who were just like me, that were going through their own identity issues. I also learned of people who were able to "fix" their physical issues with the help of surgery. The more information I learned, the easier it was for me to allow my inner "her" to be released from her hiding place. Yet, I was careful to only do that in the presence of Mark.

Through my research, I came across terms that I personally could not relate too. Some of them were words like homosexual, bisexual, and gay. I learned that they were referring to men who were attracted to other men. I knew that this was not me because I never ever identified or felt as though I was a man or a boy. I was never attracted to a man the way the research was saying that men are attracted to other men. Nor did I identify with the term bisexual.

I researched further and found stories of people, such as Lili Elbi. She was the first male to female sex change, as it was known as during her life in the 1930s. I also read about another famous person named Christine Jorgenson, who had her sex change done in Denmark in 1952. And the most well-known one of my lifetime was another outstanding individual known as Renee Richards. She had her operation in the mid-1970s.

Those stories were terrific and fueled my mind with all of the hopes, dreams, and possibilities that I, too, could be changed and fully become the girl that I knew myself to be. I knew that with my body entirely correct in gender, all would finally be right in my world.

Accumulating this knowledge created a hunger within me; a need to know and be more. I needed to understand how the surgery could be done, yet the information available to me was slim on details and limited in scope. I suddenly hit a wall in my quest, but I held to my hope, with a passion, to learn as much as I could. I took comfort in the fact that I now knew that there was a way for me to truly become who I was meant to be. I could fix all that was wrong with me.

With Mark in my life, life seemed to be less stressful. I didn't feel depressed about my identity and gender struggles anymore. Her helping me to learn to accept who I am, gave me an inner confidence that I had never felt before. It was a refreshing feeling I completely embraced.

FINALLY OUT

AT THAT TIME, MARK WAS USING THE NAME CHRISSY or Chris. We talked about this extensively and came to the decision that I needed to chose a name for myself as well. I had no idea what to call myself. I simply wanted a name that I would be comfortable with. We decided to choose my name together and, finally, after going through so many, I settled on calling myself Tina. It was a cute name and it made me feel cute as well when I said it.

Now the reality is, everyone's name has to be more than just cute. Your name should be a representation of your entire being. It should reflect everything that makes up who you are as an individual. When it is spoken or heard by others, it should be a reflection of your innermost being. You should know this by how you personally connect to the name chosen because it becomes your presentation and introduction to the world. Your name showcases who you are.

One day Chris lent me and urged me to wear a pink jumpsuit to school. We were attending Willowbrook Junior High School. I had been hesitant to wear it because it was obviously a loud color being that it was a very bright pink. Chris, supportive as always, convinced me that it looked cool and that no one would bother me about it. As a result, I braved my fears and stepped out with confidence. We had no idea that my wearing that pink jumpsuit would define both of our lives and our friendship.

Willowbrook Junior High sort of had a rough edge to it because it was located in a tough neighborhood and was filled with gang members. There were always gang fights after school and students walked around with scowls on their faces mean mugging everyone. It made you feel as if trouble would erupt at any given moment. It reminded me of how juvenile hall was. You had to always be on your guard to navigate through the negativity. You could not present yourself as a victim because you would eventually become one. In this way, the time I spent in juvie came in handy. I was not one of those soft students.

During P.E., three tough-looking boys approached me and started to ask about the sweatsuit I had on. I clearly recall my pulse began to race and my entire body became tense. My heart started beating rapidly and it felt like I was having severe chest pains. I was scared, but I knew that I could not show any type of fear because I would be eaten alive. That was my safety rule number one. In surviving confrontations when I felt threatened, fear was definitely my enemy. Knowing this, I stood my ground.

"What about it!" I snapped, looking the guy that had spoken directly in his eyes. I figured that he was the leader of the group and would be the one I had to conquer first.

Instead of him speaking, one of the other guys with a smug look on his face blurted out: "Isn't that a girl's sweatsuit?" His buddies laughed. I didn't falter in my response.

"No!" I snapped, showing my irritation. "It's unisex." They all looked confusedly at me, then at each other. Obviously, none of them had heard the term before: "What the hell is that?"

I explained, "It means that anyone can wear it, boy or girl. It is not just for one or the other." I saw in the hardening of their expressions that they didn't comprehend at all. I knew that trouble was right around the corner. They did what most guys who had no idea how to digest something they could not understand, do, they turned up the pressure and heat on me.

"Aye, man, check it out - are you funny?" One of them asked as they continued laughing amongst themselves as if what he had asked me was some sort of a joke. I knew what "funny" meant. He was asking me if I was gay. I refused to cave to the pressure, even though my heart felt like it was about to fall out of my chest. I also felt the pressure to deny who I truly was building up on the inside of me. Instead, I met their aggression head-on, knowing that it was the only way that I would gain respect from their challenge.

I instantly jumped to the level of the boy who had asked the question. "What did you say?" I snapped.

One of his friends sneered and twisted up his face showing his own aggression to match that of my own. "Nigga, you know what he said! Are you..." He flipped his hand back and forth in a feminized and derogatory way to indicate being gay.

At that moment, I felt a rage unlike anything I had ever felt before. It was an anger that rose up from the depths of my soul. I could not control it as it came forth. It had to be released and refused to be denied by me or anyone else. I didn't feel or even notice the tears that ran down my face. I felt no more pain and certainly no more pressure. I no longer felt the need to hide from the three of them or anyone else. The realization of this was like a massive volcano erupting. I exploded and snapped suddenly. "Yes! Yes, I am...So what!"

Before they could answer, I turned in defiance and walked away, feeling a sense of pride and freedom, the likes of which I never knew existed. This was the first time I had admitted what I was hiding for so long to anyone other than La' Tasha or Chris and it felt great.

My feelings of pride at standing up to those guys was short-lived as one of them threw a bottle at me. My mind ran through all of the ridicule they had thrown at me and my anger increased because they had the nerve to even question me. I immediately turned and confronted them. I was angry and ready to fight. It didn't take long before we were in an all-out brawl.

Strangely, in a way, I am grateful to them because their question forced me to be front and center with my identity in public. Although I did not identify as gay, I knew that they would never have understood the concept of a person being the wrong gender. I was barely coming to grips with the possibility of such a thing myself. And I was living it!

We fought until it was broken up by our P.E. teacher, who simply took my little frame and tossed me over his shoulder and hauled me to the principle's office. I was expelled from school.

———

WHEN I GOT BACK HOME to Momma Tee's house, I was told that my probation officer was on his way to pick me up and take me back to juvenile hall. I decided right then and there that I was not about to be going back. I was not about to let them lock me back up in that place.

I quickly packed all of my stuff and was placing it under my bed when Chris walked into the room. She was all excited. She had heard about my fight and how I had gotten kicked out of school. She wanted to know all of the details. She noticed me packing my things and asked why. I explained to her that I was going to be placed back behind bars and was refusing to let them take me. I told her that I was going to run away.

To my surprise, she started asking me not to leave her alone. She then declared that if I was going to be leaving, she was leaving with me as well. We wasted no time and after she packed her things, we snuck out the back door, jumped the fence, and ran. We never looked back. As for my property, I left it all there; more importantly, I left behind that little boy with all of his fears, doubts, and his pains. I ran with confidence that I no longer had to stay hidden.

We snuck onto a bus by entering through the back door and rode it until we reached the end of the route. We had no clue as to where we were or where to go. I just wanted to get us as far away as possible from Momma Tees and the fact that I would be going back to juvenile hall.

We ended up on Sunset Boulevard, Hollywood. The day had turned to night by this time. The sight that lay before me was unlike anything my young mind had ever seen. Even the depictions in the movies and television shows were watered down compared to what we witnessed.

I recall it being a very seedy place and definitely not a place for two young kids who were alone and had no clue as to what life was about. As we stood there wide-eyed and in awe, two prostitutes approached us. I was nervous, cold, and hungry. I had not eaten anything since the lunch period at school earlier.

Both of the two women that approached us were beautiful, and they seemed like they were concerned about us. The light-skinned one of the two began to ask us questions about ourselves and wanted to know where our parents were. "You should not be out here on these streets alone." She said, looking hard at us. "How old are you two?"

Chris was the one who answered and did most of the talking. And, instead of answering her question, said, "We'll be fine." The tone was very dismissive.

The prostitute brushed off the way Chris answered her and continued giving us advice. "Y'all need to go home. This is no safe place for kids. You can get hurt hanging out here." She looked at both of us with genuine concern. Yet, although her expression held concern, it also held suspicion. After a moment, she continued. "Well, y'all be careful out here. There is a lot of creeps that hang out here." She and her friend set off to go and do their business for the night, leaving only the scent of their perfume thick in the air.

Chris and I took off walking down the street trying to take in all of the sights and sounds at once. We came across a Thrifty's store and went inside. We strolled up and down the isles shoplifting items of food that we ate as we walked through the store. We also stole everything Chris thought we would need. We stole dresses, heels, purses, along with makeup. Then, we waited until the perfect opportunity came and quickly left.

Next, we went into a bowling ally where Chris and I changed into our new clothes. For me, it was like shedding my old skin and putting on a new one. Chris applied makeup to both of our faces, which made me feel pretty, but also made my skin feel weird, being that it was the first time I ever felt it on my face.

Trying to walk in a pair of five or six-inch mule pumps at eleven years old, for me at least, was also weird and unreal. I could not even stand up straight and had to bend my knees as I wobbled, praying that I did not fall flat on my face.

Oh, but Chris, she walked in those shoes like a supermodel strutting in all her glory down a runway. I was both amazed and envious of her sass, grace, and beauty. She moved as if she had been born with a pair of heels on.

Although everything was awkward for me, I was so happy. I was finally OUT!!! I was living freely as a girl.

It was the most liberating thing I had ever experienced. The friendship that Chris and I created and bonded is still one that we share to this day. It is a sisterhood formed out of the depths of despair and forged by the hardships of a confused life. It developed and is still held by these profound connections.

WHO'S TIFFANY

YEARS LATER, WHILE IN JUVENILE HALL, YES I eventually went back there, I ran into an old friend from the neighborhood that I had grown up in. He recognized me and was shocked to see me living as a girl. He called me by my childhood name, which was Papa. When he was sure that it was me, he threatened to tell my parents that I was dressing and looking like a girl. We began to argue and it became so heated that we ended up in a serious physical altercation. We happened to be in a church service and became so disruptive that we were removed.

In the end, he did exactly what he said he was going to do when he returned home. He told any and everyone he knew about me. I was by then, permanently living in a group home located in Hollywood, known as Hudson House. It was run by the Gay and Lesbian Community Center.

One day, my probation officer contacted me by phone and let me know that my family was trying to get in contact with me. He gave me a phone number to call, then he hung up. I was confused and had a dilemma on my hands. What was I going to do? I had not spoken to anyone or seen them in quite some time.

Now, this was around 1982 and I was living as a teenage girl with confidence and in no way was I going to be forced by anyone to live my life as a boy ever again. I knew if given a chance, my family would do just that and try and make me live as they wished for me too.

I was conflicted in that I wanted to forget my past, my family included, yet I missed my mother and my siblings. I contemplated calling them for a few days and eventually worked up the nerve to do so.

I will never forget it. I was standing on the corner of Santa Monica and Vine street, at a payphone. I nervously dialed the number my probation officer had given me. The phone on the other end rang. Every fiber of my being wanted to quickly hang up before it was answered. Fear ate at me. I was tempted to take off running. But, before my nerves could get the better of me, the phone was picked up. It was my Aunt Linda who had answered.

"Hello?" "Hello? Who is this?" She replied. I could tell that she recognized my voice as she suddenly said, "Papa? Hey, how are you? We ain't heard from you in so long. We heard that you were living in Hollywood. What's in Hollywood?"

I took a moment to clear my throat that was suddenly as dry as the desert. "Yeah, it's me. Hi, Aunt Linda. How is everybody doing? I miss you all too. Yes, I live here in Hollywood and I am doing fine." I gave all of the standard answers to her questions and made them as generic as I could. We ended up talking for a while, then she, out of the blue, spoke on what I knew was coming.

"Papa, let me ask you something." She said. "Who is Tiffany?"

In that second, I could have been shot by a bullet and would not have noticed because I grew instantly numb. I was shocked beyond my ability to describe. In 1979, while in juvenile hall, I changed my name from Tina to Tiffany. I came by that name one day while looking through a Vogue magazine and saw an ad for the famous store chain.

Seeing the name was an instant connection for me. I knew that I was Tiffany. There was no denying that that was my name and no other one would fit so perfectly. In truth, I felt that the name chose me just as much as I chose it.

While on the phone, I suddenly became very guarded. I answered by saying, "I don't know. Who is Tiffany?" At that moment, I realized that fear of my family's rejection was still prevalent in my heart. I understood that it had a tight grip on my spirit. It had me denying myself and that alone was something that I had told myself countless times that I was never going to do again. Even still, I knew that Aunt Linda knew that I was lying. She just wanted me to say that I knew. But I just couldn't.

"I don't know. That is why I asked you who she was." As I continued denying myself, I could feel the distance growing between the two of us. But, I was committed to my course and did not back down.

"Well, I just thought maybe you had something that you wanted to tell me." She didn't hesitate to say. There was a pause as she waited for my response, so I spoke.

"Uh-uh." I quickly said. Little did I know that those would be the last words that would be spoken between any member of my family and me for many years to come.

GENDER REASSIGNMENT SURGERY

As time went on, I came to know that I wanted to transition from male to female by having gender reassignment surgery. Daily, I had been living as a girl since 1978. I remember seeing others that I thought were like me, but some big differences stood. Many of the other girls were only seen at night. They were "clockable" - either because they had trouble passing as female during the day or they slept all day because they were prostituting at night.

Now, this was in the 1980s and everything was big and bigger, loud and louder, in hair, fashion, and makeup. Many of the girls that I watched, emulated, and was learning from were of the bigger and louder sort. They were always wearing huge wigs that looked heavy and outrageous. They wore makeup that was ever too much and too loud - 'drag queen' like in an overdone sort of way. Even still, to me, it was beautiful on most of the girls.

Although these were the people that I was hanging out with, they did not present the identity that I identified my image with. Over the top was not exactly how I saw myself. A gay friend of mine, and a drag queen, saw me early one morning and said, "Ms. Tiffany, I didn't know that you had hair under that wig."

I was a bit confused by his statement but nonetheless answered, "Yes, I have hair. Why? Doesn't everybody have hair?'" I continued looking at him, confused.

Instead of answering directly, he began to examine my hair and makeup, like a stylist figuring out the perfect look. "I don't know why you wear those wigs all the time cause you have really nice hair. You look more like a woman without all of that war paint and that helmet that you live in." He was referring to both the wigs and the makeup. "That stuff is for someone like me who does shows, comes home, then takes it all off. It is all an illusion that we are selling. It is all an act." He continued, "I see you really are trying to "live" as a woman! If that is so, then you need to get into what they are giving. You need to be looking like they are looking and be natural as you are right now. Because right now, you are giving me fish! You are giving me true tuna! You're looking like a real woman!"

One day, I took his advice and caught the 210 bus, which goes down Crenshaw Boulevard. I saw a lot of African American women walking in and out of storefronts, hair salons, and running their daily errands. To my eyes, they were beautiful, stylish, and wore their individualities with a look of visible confidence.

"Yes," I said softly to myself. "This is what I see myself giving. This is the kind of woman I aspire to be." From that moment on, I sought to make it a reality and lived it. There were no more wigs that were fit for a drag queen for me, no more caked-on makeup either. In fact, I started wearing almost no makeup at all. I just let everything about myself be natural, unforced, and unexaggerated. I started feeling more and more complete and authentic.

Yet, even though I was living out my truth in a convincing fashion, I still had a nagging feeling of being incomplete within my body. In 1984, at the age of eighteen, I started my first ever hormonal treatment, also known as hormone replacement therapy. This felt like a sort of right of passage to me as I daily anticipated witnessing the feminization of my body that I dreamt was possible. I was beyond myself with joy about the development of my breast, hips, softening of my skin, and everything feminine.

I remember my first estrogen injection and my first bottle of Premarin pills. Yes, the estrogen eventually turned my body feminine. I now had beautiful, full-sized breasts, softly curved contours to my body, and my skin was soft and hairless. My face was more defined, as well. I believe that the estrogen had worked well in helping me see my body becoming more of that of a woman's; nonetheless, I still felt and feel incomplete. Even though I have lived as a woman for forty-one years, this pain is still present in my life.

I knew that gender-affirming surgery, aka sexual reassignment surgery, was the only thing that would permanently heal and soothe my pain. For most of the women like myself, having this surgery is the Holy Grail. This was the act to complete me by restoring the body and genitalia of a woman to my soul.

I started pursuing my goal of having the surgery. Now let me say this, I have never thought of this as something that I wanted. This has always been an intense need for me. There cannot be a single doubt about this point that I am making. I have never doubted that the surgery was my lifeline. I need this surgery and I need the love of my family. I have been deprived of both things for far too long. I need for my family to know that this issue I was dealing with is real and not some "sexual perversion" that they may have thought or believed it to be. I want everyone to know that for me, this has always been about my gender identity and not about sex.

Many people may not know or even understand the anguish of not living your complete self, but it was so hard that I, on several occasions, as both a child and as a young adult, contemplated committing suicide. I know that having surgery is the only thing in my life that will bring me a sense of peace.

———

In 2015, while at Mule Creek State Prison, I witnessed inmate Michelle-Lael Norsworthy win her case to receive sexual reassignment surgery. This was a huge legal victory. For a judge to order the Department of Corrections to provide an incarcerated transgender person the operation was unprecedented. The ruling applied to any transwoman in state prison who had been diagnosed with gender dysphoria. If it is found that the surgery is necessary, the prison could not deny the operation.

With this in mind and with hopes high, I applied for the surgery by placing a written 7362 medical request. Later I was called by my primary care physician to the medical office and they put my request through to the officials who were in charge of handling such requests.

A few weeks later, I was seen by a medical doctor who interviewed me and only wanted to know my medical history. He submitted his information. I was then seen by a psychologist who was assigned to interview me. She only wanted to know of my life as a transwoman. After I gave her my story, she submitted her information. A few months later, I was called to the mental health department and was told that I had been denied my request for gender-affirming surgery.

Needless to say I was devastated and I was confused as to why I had been turned down. I was told I was being medically treated with the proper care through the estrogen treatment and that was enough to help me cope with my dysphoria.

I was pissed! I was angrier than I had ever been. How could they even render such a decision about my life without even meeting with me to learn first hand what my needs were? The people that I had met with felt that I was the right candidate for the surgery. I was crushed beyond measure and felt that the decision and the entire system was unfair. I wanted to lash out at everyone, but I restrained myself. I could resubmit my request for the surgery a year from the date that I had been denied.

I have been knocked down, embarrassed, bruised, harassed, and denied for so many years and in so many circumstances in life. I endured and forced myself to face them all head-on. I was determined to do the same with this new obstacle.

l went through the same process as before, yet this time, it came with some differences. When I was seen by the medical doctor, this time, he did a full and complete examination of my body. He also asked me a lot more questions.

When I saw the psychologist for the second time, I told her that nothing had changed. I was still seeking to have surgery to completely become who I am. She advised me of the procedure and the adverse possibilities of having the surgery. I explained to her that if I woke after the surgery with the genitalia of a woman and then flatlined five minutes later, I would have lived a complete life because I would have died complete. I told her that it was important for me to have the surgery because I did not want to die in an incomplete body. She told me that I should write a letter to those who approved or denied the requests, which I did, and she submitted it along with her report.

———

ON MAY 7, 2018, I received news that changed my entire life, I was approved to have sexual reassignment surgery. Six months later, in November 2018, I had my first consultation with my surgeon, Dr. Angela Rodriguez. She agreed that I was a good candidate for the surgery and recommended immediate hair removal from my genitals before the surgery. On January 23, 2019, I began electrolysis to have the hair permanently removed from my phallus. I am happy and I feel like my complete self is about to revealed and will finally be whole. I look back at the struggling little girl that I was and say to her, be strong sister, you are worth fighting for. You matter. You exist. You have a beautiful purpose in this world. You are going to be all right.

Even with such a decision as this, and with me finally getting everything I know that I need in my life for my completeness, it also still brings me loss. Some cannot or will not want to understand what I have been going through and why there is such a dire and pressing need within me to have this surgery. They may find both me and the surgery unacceptable. I cannot and would not ever try to make anyone accept me against their will. I want to be freely loved and freely accepted for who I am by those individuals who choose to love me.

If losing loved ones is the outcome of my surgery and the pursuit of my own happiness and completeness, then that is a loss I am more than willing to accept. Yes, it will be painful and my heart will mourn, but it will not be more painful than the burden I have had to carry for most of my life. Plus, I will be happy. And for my happiness, I will not apologize to anyone!

Not only is this huge in my personal life regarding my completeness, but it is also huge on a grander scale in that I am the first African American transgender woman to be approved for sexual reassignment surgery by the California Department of Corrections and Rehabilitation. This is monumental for other trans women of color, who are in similar situations, to see that we are now being given these opportunities. To be the first to receive approval without the courts ordering the corrections system to perform the surgery will have a ripple effect that may impact the lives of transwomen who feel as if they will never have the chance to become complete.

I look at all the women who made it possible for me to be in this position and I thank them for their sacrifices and their persistence in fighting for what they knew to be a "need" in them. They, Michelle-Lael Norsworthy and Shiloh Heavenly Quine, went through hell being judged, criticized, and ridiculed, to bring their reality to fruition. A lot of what they endured was both brutal and unfair, which makes me appreciate even more the privacy being given to my own situation. I am happy that no media attention or hoopla is surrounding me as it was with them. This is about my body and not about some sensationalized story to be exploited and made a spectacle of.

Now I will confess that starting the electrolysis and having my hair removed has not been a pleasant. The hair shafts on my body are shocked and burnt with heat to eradicate any new hair growth. It is done by using a needle-like probe that is inserted into the follicle and then the hair is plucked out. It has worked well and has my genital area smooth.

I still have to continue this procedure for a little while longer. The skin from this area will be used to construct my vagina during the vaginoplasty surgery. I don't complain or ask for any stoppage of the procedure because I have fought long and hard for this and I want everything to be right. I don't expect anything on my journey to be easy or be without some sort of pain and difficulty.

I also will have to go through painful dilation of the vagina after my surgery is complete. I can already imagine how that is going to hurt. I will need to insert a vibrator-like object into the vagina to lengthen and widen the canal. Even so, I am delighted and ready to face it head-on. I want my new vagina to function normally and naturally. This is my new beginning and I am as happy as a child who wakes up on Christmas morning to open up her new gift.

COME WHAT MAY

I AM THANKFUL TO BE GIVEN THIS OPPORTUNITY TO share my journey and hope that my story will help to shed some light on the path for others who feel confused and afraid. I say to you all, do not be afraid to be who you know that you are. Allow yourself the chance to be free and I encourage you to shine brightly in your very own truth. You will not regret it; however, you will regret it if you hide and suffer needlessly.

Being able to tell my story had been very therapeutic for me. I have been able to let all of the pains of my past go, and not having to hold them, or carry them any longer is so refreshing. I say to you, just let go! I refuse to go through my new life, holding on to all of the past baggage. I am detached from it.

Lastly, I wish to say how delighted I was to receive a letter from my friend Mark Anthony Henderson Rainey, aka Ms. Chrissy, in 2015. He is happily living as a gay man. In his letter, he stated that he had always admired me because he knew that I was/am a real woman. He said, "I knew you were serious about who you are. I'm so proud of you and want you to know I've always looked up to you."

For me, hearing those words from my best friend who I know helped me free myself and let me be the woman I am today, was a culmination of my life's journey. I want to say thank you, Chrissy, I love you, dearly.

I recall our lives together as an adventure that was something one would think was made from the movies or a television show. The two of us packed a lot of life, love, adventure, pain, heartache, heartbreaks, dangers, comforts, and excitement into the years we shared together.

Of course, we had our ups and downs as any family does, yet no matter what, we have always overcome any issues that arose. I count that friendship as one of my greatest blessings.

I have had many opportunities in my life to be success-ful. I have been blessed with some very good jobs. I have taken advantage of the opportunity to obtain my high school diploma. I have also earned college credits in both business and psychology. Yet in spite of this, I have failed to grow in those opportunities.

Why? This is an excellent question. I just was not settled enough in my own life to hold solidly to any of my achievements. But, even so, I was never shy about giving myself any chance that came across my path. But, as I have mentioned, and it is so significant to who I am, it bears saying once more, I have always believed that life is what you make of it. It is your responsibility to make the best of things, good or bad.

I have taken all of the lows I have experienced in life and used them as teaching tools to learn from. Each hardship I have endured has made me a better person than I was before. I have entirely accepted responsibility for the wrongs I have done to others and I have moved on from them. Yet, I have not forgotten anything I have done. I do not make any excuses. I have made peace with and forgiven myself so that I may move forward into my future with a clear conscience. This gives me a sense of confidence about the decisions I make moving forward.

I guess that I am mostly asked by others, what do I think I am going to feel after having my reassignment surgery. I have said many things in response to the question, but to honestly sum it up, I will feel relief. I will feel euphoric. Yet the one thing I want to do immediately once my body has healed enough for me to move around is, pull up my panties, then quickly pull them down again, then back up once more. The knowledge of knowing that I can now do this without having to tuck myself because the male genitalia is no longer there will be blissful. To know that I will no longer have to adjust anything, or ever hide anything again will be a dream come true. My genitalia will no longer be an illusion. I will have a real vagina. I pray that everything will go well so that my "coin purse" will be as perfect as possible. (LOL)

The first fifty years of my life are now behind me. I am working on a new fifty full of positivity. No negativity is allowed to linger and settle in. I'm living for today, tomorrow, and beyond. The past is just that, the past.

EAST OAKLAND TIMES

The East Oakland Times, LLC (EOT) is a multi-media publication based in the San Francisco Bay Area. Founded by chief editor, Tio MacDonald. EOT has at its core three principles: the principle of the dignity of life, the principle of liberty, and the principle of tolerance. EOT supports the flourishing of civilization through the peace found by honoring these three stated principles.

Support the EOT by purchasing EOT produced e-books, print books, and audiobooks!

www.eastoaklandtimes.com

———

Titles Include:
My Crime Series - The First Offense: Five True Crime Stories From California Inmates
3P's - Pleasure, Pain, & Passion

Learning Curve: An Introduction to (Death Row Inmate) Johnny D. Miles' Collage Art, Poetry, & Mind Striving for Redemption
Tio MacDonald Interviews Series

———

Stay positive & productive!

Tio MacDonald
Chief Editor